can you find
Followers of Jesus?

Introducing Your Child to Disciples

Written by **Philip D. Gallery**
Illustrated by **Janet L. Harlow**

ST. ANTHONY MESSENGER PRESS

Cincinnati, Ohio

NOVALIS

Written by Philip D. Gallery
Illustrated by Janet L. Harlow
Cover and book design by settingPace and Mary Alfieri

Copyright © 2000, Philip D. Gallery and Janet L. Harlow

Published in the United States by
St. Anthony Messenger Press
1615 Republic St., Cincinnati, OH 45210-1298

ISBN 0-86716-388-7

Published in Canada by Novalis
49 Front St. E, 2nd Floor
Toronto, Ontario M5E 1B3 Canada
1-800-387-7164

Canadian Cataloguing in Publication Data

Gallery, Philip D.
Can you find followers of Jesus? : introducing your child
to the disciples
ISBN 2-89507-120-9

1. Apostles. 2. Bible, N.T.-Study and teaching.
I. Harlow, Janet L. II. Title.

BS2440.G34 2000 225.9'22 C00-900911-6

Printed and bound in the U.S.A. by Worzalla.

Contents

Introduction

In the first two books of the "Search and Learn" series, **Can You Find Bible Heroes?** and **Can You Find Jesus?**, we introduced children to the stories and messages of the Old and New Testaments of the Bible. In **Can You Find Followers of Jesus?** we will introduce your child to God's call to follow him—to discipleship.

From the beginning, God has called people to follow and obey him. In the Old Testament, God told Adam and Eve not to eat the fruit, Abraham to leave his homeland, Noah to build an Ark, Moses to help lead his people to the Promised Land and Jonah to bring the word of God to the people of Nineveh (see Search 1).

The New Testament story of obedience began when God asked Mary to be the mother of his son, Jesus, and she agreed to follow where God was leading her. Jesus himself came into the world in obedience to the will of his Father in heaven, to deliver God's message to us personally (see Search 3). To help him deliver God's message, Jesus picked many followers and sent them out to spread his message to the world (see Search 4). In his life and death, Jesus provided people with the perfect example for following God.

After Jesus returned to his Father in heaven, the followers of Jesus continued to spread his message (see Searches 5, 8 and 10). They taught God's message to many people who did not know Jesus while he was in the world. These new followers of Jesus, even though they had never met Jesus, helped spread God's message even farther (see Search 12).

Before they died, those who had known Jesus wrote the New Testament of the Bible to pass on to all people of all time the message that God had delivered to them (see Search 11). For the past two thousand years those who have read the New Testament have helped the followers of Jesus spread God's message to the world (see Search 13). It is now our turn to spread God's message. Our book is designed to help the young, and not so young, see their place in God's plan to have his message spread to all the people in the world.

Just as those who knew Jesus needed his guidance in learning what God wanted them to do, so your children need guidance from you and the other adults in their lives, if they are to learn what God expects of them. When young children explore the pictures in this book, Jesus and many of the men and women who have followed him through the years will come alive for them. As you guide older children through the text on each page, you will be helping them see what it means to be a follower of Jesus. To help you develop in your child a deeper understanding of what it means to follow Jesus, we have provided a Parent's Guide for each picture beginning on page 32. In addition, the meanings of key words in italics are given in the Glossary on page 39. Finally, each page contains several silly things meant to amuse those of you who are called upon repeatedly to share this book with the young people in your life.

We hope each of you who looks at and reads our book will come a bit closer to understanding what Jesus meant when he looked at Peter and said simply, "Follow me!"

Philip Gallery and Janet Harlow

Hidden in Every Picture

These ten things are hidden in every picture. Nine of them hold a special meaning in the lives of Jesus and his followers. The tenth one is you—and each of us.

 **Angels** are beings created by God to share the joy of heaven. In the Old Testament, angels guarded the entrance to Eden (see Genesis 3:23-24), wrestled with Jacob (see Genesis 32:23-31) and served God in many other ways. In the New Testament, angels told Mary she would be the mother of God (see Search 1: God Calls Us to Follow Him), announced the birth of Jesus (see Luke 2:8-14), told Joseph to take the baby Jesus into Egypt (see Matthew 2:13-15), and freed Peter from prison (see Acts 5:17-21).

 The **bag of gold** is a symbol for the power of the world (see Search 2: Jesus Calls His Disciples). Too often, people spend their lives building up earthly treasures rather than following God. Jesus often warned that people who care too much for the things of the world may be too busy to find time for God (see Matthew 19:21-23).

 The **Bible** is the instruction manual for life. The Old Testament was written by the Jewish ancestors of Jesus to explain God's relationship to his chosen people. The New Testament was written by the followers of Jesus (see Search 11: The Followers of Jesus Write His Story) to make sure that those of us who never met Jesus would know what he wants us to do. If you ever wish God would talk to you, pick up the Bible and he will.

 The **cross** reminds us of Jesus dying on a cross to save us (see Search 5: Jesus Sends the Holy Spirit to Help His Followers). In dying for us, Jesus taught us that, like him, we need to obey God. He also showed us how much he loves us.

 The **fish** stands for Christians. Jesus told his followers that he would make them fishers of people (see Search 2: Jesus Calls His Disciples), meaning that his followers were to go all over the world and tell everyone about Jesus. When the followers of Jesus had to hide from people who wanted to hurt them, they used the fish as their secret sign.

The **rock** represents Peter, the first leader of Jesus' Church (see Search 10: Peter Carries God's Message to the Gentiles and Matthew 16:18-19). In the time of Jesus, rock was the strongest foundation you could find for a building. Jesus' Church stands on the shoulders of Peter, while Peter stands on the shoulders of Jesus.

The **scroll** (see Search 3: Jesus Gives His Message to His Followers and Search 11: The Followers of Jesus Write His Story) represents the written word of God. In the time of Jesus, and in Old Testament times, most writing was done on scrolls. For the Jewish people, the Old Testament scrolls contain the sacred teachings of God. Christians should look on the Bible, both the Old and New Testaments, in the same way.

The **sheep** (see Search 4: Jesus Sends His Followers Before Him) represents the lost people of God. Jesus referred to himself as the good shepherd who had come to look for his lost sheep (see Luke 15:3-7 and John 10:1-16).

The **tongue of fire** is the form the Holy Spirit took when it entered the Apostles and other followers of Jesus on Pentecost (see Search 5: Jesus Sends the Holy Spirit to Help His Followers).

The **child** in modern clothes in each picture shows that it isn't just people from the time of Jesus who should be his followers, but that people from all times, including our own, should follow him (see Search 13: The Message of Jesus Is Passed From Follower to Follower).

SEARCH 1
God Calls Us to Follow Him

From the beginning of time, God has asked people to *obey* him. In the *Old Testament* of the Bible, God told many people what he wanted them to do. Some obeyed him and some didn't. Finally God sent Jesus to teach us what God wants us to do.

God told Adam and Eve not to eat the fruit from a tree in the Garden of Eden. But Adam and Eve disobeyed God and ate the fruit, so God made them leave the Garden of Eden. **CAN YOU FIND ADAM AND EVE?**

Later God told Abraham to leave his land and go to a new land he had never seen. Abraham took his family and did what God told him to do. **CAN YOU FIND ABRAHAM?**

The Lord told Jonah to go to *Nineveh* and tell the people they must stop doing bad things. Jonah didn't want to go, so he got on a ship and tried to hide from God. **CAN YOU FIND JONAH?**

The angel Gabriel was sent by God to Mary. He told her, "You will have a son, and you will name him Jesus." Mary answered, "I am the servant of the Lord; let it be with me according to your word." **CAN YOU FIND MARY?**

When Jesus was twelve, he went to the Temple in Jerusalem. After Mary and Joseph found him, Mary said, "Your father and I have been searching for you." He answered, "Did you not know that I must be in my Father's house?" **CAN YOU FIND THE YOUNG JESUS?**

When Jesus was *baptized*, a voice came from *heaven* and said, "This is my Son, the Beloved, with whom I am well pleased." **CAN YOU FIND JESUS?**

SEARCH 2
Jesus Calls His Disciples

Jesus came to deliver a message from God to all the people on earth. Because the world is a very big place with lots of people, Jesus asked people to help him deliver God's message. The people who helped Jesus were his followers. They were also called *disciples*.

Jesus was standing by the *Sea of Galilee* when he saw two fishermen named Peter and Andrew. "Follow me," he said to them, "and I will make you fishers of men." The fishermen immediately followed Jesus. **CAN YOU FIND PETER AND ANDREW?**

Next, Jesus saw Philip. "Follow me," Jesus said to him. Philip found his friend Nathanael and told him that he had found the *Messiah*. After this, Philip and Nathanael followed Jesus. **CAN YOU FIND PHILIP AND NATHANAEL?**

Later, Jesus met a man named Matthew. Matthew was a tax collector. Jesus said to him, "Follow me." Matthew got up and did as he was told. **CAN YOU FIND MATTHEW?**

One day a man asked Jesus what he had to do to be God's friend. Jesus told the man to keep the *Ten Commandments*, give his money to the poor, and follow him. Because he had a lot of money, the man didn't want to give it away. So he didn't follow Jesus. **CAN YOU FIND THE RICH MAN?**

After praying, Jesus called his disciples and chose twelve of them to be his Apostles. Their names are Peter, Andrew, James, John, Philip, Bartholomew, Matthew, Thomas, Simon, James, the son of Alphaeus, Judas, the son of James, and Judas Iscariot. **CAN YOU FIND THE TWELVE APOSTLES?**

SEARCH 3
Jesus Gives His Message to His Followers

After Jesus had chosen his disciples, he told them that he had been sent by God. To show his disciples that God had sent him, Jesus performed many *miracles*. Then Jesus told his disciples the messages God wanted them to deliver to all the people in the world.

Jesus unrolled the *scroll* of the *prophet* Isaiah and read, "The *spirit of the Lord* is upon me. The Lord has sent me to bring good news to the poor." **CAN YOU FIND JESUS?**

Then a man asked Jesus, "Teacher, which *commandment* is the greatest?" Jesus answered, "You shall love the Lord your God and you shall love your neighbor as yourself." **CAN YOU FIND THE MAN?**

One day Jesus told a group of people, "You are my friends if you do what I command. I command you to love one another." **CAN YOU FIND THE FRIENDS OF JESUS?**

Then Jesus told his followers, "When you pray say, 'Our Father who art in heaven, *hallowed* be thy name.'" **CAN YOU FIND THE CHILDREN PRAYING?**

Next, Jesus taught that you should invite the poor, disabled and blind when you have a party. "You will be repaid by God for your kindness," Jesus said. **CAN YOU FIND THE PARTY-GOERS?**

At another time Jesus said, "If anyone hurts you, even if he hurts you seven times a day, you are to forgive him." **CAN YOU FIND THE FORGIVING CHILD?**

One day Jesus asked Peter, "Do you love me?" Peter answered, "Yes, Lord, you know that I love you." Then Jesus said to Peter, "Feed my sheep." **CAN YOU FIND PETER?**

SEARCH 4

Jesus Sends His Followers Before Him

Once the followers of Jesus understood his message, he sent them, two at a time, to many of the cities he planned to visit. Jesus wanted his followers to tell everyone about him. He gave them many instructions to follow. He also gave them the power to cure the sick.

Jesus called the twelve Apostles together and told them to go all over the countryside. "Tell the people," he said, "that the *Kingdom of God* is near." **CAN YOU FIND JESUS?**

Then Jesus told his *Apostles*, "Go to the *lost sheep* of the *House of Israel* and teach them all I have taught you." **CAN YOU FIND THE LOST SHEEP?**

Next, Jesus told the Apostles not to take money, food or clothes with them. He said the people the Apostles helped would take care of them. **CAN YOU FIND THE TWELVE APOSTLES?**

Finally Jesus warned the Apostles, "I am sending you out as sheep among wolves. But do not worry about what you are to say. God, your Father, will tell you what to say." **CAN YOU FIND THE WOLVES?**

After sending his Apostles, Jesus sent thirty-six more pairs of followers to every town he was going to visit. "Those who hear you, hear me," he told them, "and those who reject you, reject me." **CAN YOU FIND THE FOLLOWERS AROUND JESUS?**

SEARCH 5
Jesus Sends the Holy Spirit to Help His Followers

Jesus followed his disciples around the countryside teaching people to do what God wanted them to do. Then some people killed Jesus. After Jesus died, he rose from the dead and returned to his Father in heaven.

Before he returned to heaven, Jesus told his Apostles, "You will receive power when the *Holy Spirit* comes down on you. Then you are to teach all the people in the world about me." **CAN YOU FIND JESUS?**

While they were waiting for the Holy Spirit, Jesus' Apostles replaced Judas, who had been an Apostle until he helped the people who killed Jesus. They chose Mathias to replace Judas. **CAN YOU FIND MATHIAS?**

A few days later, a wind came into the room where the Apostles were gathered, and *tongues of fire* appeared. The tongues of fire split and came to rest on each of the Apostles, who were filled with the Holy Spirit. **CAN YOU FIND THE TONGUES OF FIRE?**

Then the Apostles went into the streets to teach the people about Jesus. People from different countries heard the Apostles speaking in their languages. **CAN YOU FIND THE APOSTLES?**

Then Peter stood up and said, "All of you listen to me. Jesus was a man sent to you from God. Therefore you must be baptized in the name of Jesus Christ." **CAN YOU FIND PETER?**

Because the Apostles needed help, they chose seven more men to help them. **CAN YOU FIND THE SEVEN MEN?**

GO TO JAIL
GO DIRECTLY TO JAIL

PETER

DAMASCUS

CEMENT CEMENT
CEMENT
CEMENT

SEARCH 6
Jesus Calls Saul to Be His Follower

As soon as the followers of Jesus started to teach what Jesus had told them to teach, the leaders of the country became afraid. What scared them most was his followers' claims that Jesus was the Son of God and therefore a king whom everyone should follow. To stop the followers of Jesus from teaching, the leaders attacked them and even killed some of them.

The leaders arrested Peter and asked him, "By what power or in whose name do you teach?" Peter answered, "We teach in the name of Jesus Christ, whom God raised from the dead." **CAN YOU FIND PETER?**

Stephen, another follower of Jesus, was also arrested for teaching about Jesus. The leaders dragged him out of the city and began to stone him. **CAN YOU FIND STEPHEN?**

Then Saul, one of the leaders, began going from house to house, dragging men and women out and throwing them into jail. **CAN YOU FIND SAUL?**

Later Saul traveled to *Damascus* to arrest more followers of Jesus. On the way a light from the sky blinded him and he heard a voice say, "Saul, why do you attack me?" "Who are you?" Saul asked. "I am Jesus," the voice replied. **CAN YOU FIND THE BLIND SAUL?**

After Saul reached Damascus, a follower of Jesus came to him and said, "I have been sent by the Lord Jesus to help you recover your sight." Suddenly, scales fell from his eyes and Saul could see. He became a follower of Jesus. **CAN YOU FIND THE SEEING SAUL?**

 Saul stayed in Damascus and began to teach that Jesus was the Son of God. **CAN YOU FIND THE PREACHING SAUL?**

SEARCH 7

The Followers of Jesus Travel to Antioch

Because the followers of Jesus were being attacked in Jerusalem, many of them decided to go to *Antioch*. When they had questions about how best to follow Jesus, they sent messengers to Peter, who was still in Jerusalem, for the answers.

 Some of the followers of Jesus who were in Antioch taught the message of Jesus to the Jewish people living there. **CAN YOU FIND THE FOLLOWER OF JESUS TEACHING THE JEWS?**

Other followers of Jesus in Antioch began to teach the Greeks about Jesus. Because the Greeks weren't Jews, the Church leaders in Jerusalem sent Barnabas, a disciple of Jesus, to Antioch to see what was happening. **CAN YOU FIND THE FOLLOWER OF JESUS TEACHING THE GREEKS?**

Barnabas was so impressed by what he saw that he went to get Saul. Together they taught many people about Jesus. At this time the followers of Jesus were called Christians. **CAN YOU FIND THE CHRISTIANS?**

Many Jewish followers of Jesus thought the Greeks and other non-Jewish followers of Jesus should obey all the Jewish laws. The Church leaders in Jerusalem sent two messengers to Antioch to say these followers would only have to obey some of the Jewish laws. **CAN YOU FIND THE TWO MESSENGERS?**

When it came time to spread the message of Jesus beyond Antioch, the Holy Spirit picked Barnabas and Saul for this work. After everyone prayed, the Church leaders laid their hands on Barnabas and Saul, who then sailed off to teach about Jesus. **CAN YOU FIND BARNABAS AND SAUL?**

ROME

PETER

PHILIPPI

ATHENS

CORINTH

MALTA

SEARCH 8
Paul Spreads God's Message

Because it was still unsafe for the followers of Jesus to be in Jerusalem, Paul, who used to be called Saul, decided to travel around and teach about Jesus to the Jews who were living outside of Jerusalem. On the trip, Paul was accompanied by Barnabas.

Paul and Barnabas first went to Cyprus. There they met a magician who was turning people away from God. Paul said to the magician, "For a time you will be blind," and he was. **CAN YOU FIND THE BLIND MAGICIAN?**

Next they went to Lystra. They found a man who had never been able to walk. Paul said to him, "Stand up." The man jumped up and walked around. **CAN YOU FIND THE CURED MAN?**

Then Paul went to Philippi. He was put in prison, but an earthquake broke open the prison doors. The jailer was afraid, so Paul told him, "Believe in the Lord Jesus and you will be saved." **CAN YOU FIND THE JAILER?**

Paul then went to Athens, where he found an *altar* to an unknown god. Paul told the people this unknown god was Jesus, the real God who made the world. **CAN YOU FIND THE ALTAR?**

After that, Paul went to Corinth. Many people who heard him believed in Jesus and were baptized. In a dream, the Lord said to Paul, "Do not be afraid, for I am with you." **CAN YOU FIND THE DREAMING PAUL?**

Paul returned to Jerusalem, but was arrested and put on a ship to Rome. The ship wrecked on an island, where Paul was bitten by a snake. **CAN YOU FIND THE SNAKE?**

At last Paul arrived in Rome. He told the Jewish leaders, "I have done nothing against our people, yet I am a prisoner." **CAN YOU FIND THE PREACHING PAUL?**

21

SEARCH 9

Many Women Answer the Call of Jesus to Follow Him

Beginning with Mary agreeing to be his mother, many women answered Jesus' call to follow him. In the time of Jesus, it was unusual for men and women to gather together in public, especially in religious settings. But Jesus called women to follow him because he wanted to make it clear that he had come to bring God's message to all people—men and women, Jews and non-Jews.

Among the women present at the *crucifixion* of Jesus were his mother, his mother's sister, and Mary Magdalene. **CAN YOU FIND THE MOTHER OF JESUS?**

After Jesus had been in the tomb for three days, Mary Magdalene and some of his other women followers went to the tomb. There they were met by an angel who told them that Jesus had been raised from the dead. Suddenly Jesus appeared to them and said, "Peace! Do not be afraid." **CAN YOU FIND MARY MAGDALENE?**

After Jesus was raised from the dead, many women came to be his followers. Tabitha was one of these. Because she loved Jesus, she did many good things and helped many people. **CAN YOU FIND TABITHA?**

Sometime later Peter was arrested and thrown into prison. An angel helped him escape and he went to the house of Mary, the mother of John, where many followers of Jesus were praying. **CAN YOU FIND MARY, THE MOTHER OF JOHN?**

World News

AN ALLEGED ANGEL ACCOMPLICE ASSISTS ARRESTED APOSTLE .... AVOIDS AUTHORITIES!

WOMEN CONTINUE TO COME TO THE FOLLOWERS OF JESUS TO BE BAPTIZED.

TROPHY FISH CAUGHT FRIDAY !!!

OBITUARIES

WOMAN WHO WITHHOLDS WEALTH, REAPS WRATH !!!

Thought for the Day...
"A woman who fears the Lord is to be praised."
—Proverbs 31:30

for Women

FOLLOWER REWARDED !!!

JOPPA NEWS: TABITHA, A WOMAN OF
GOOD DEEDS HAS BEEN HONORED.

~~ ~~~ ~~~ ~~~ ~~~ ~~~
~~ ~~~ ~~ ~~~ ~~~ ~~
~~ ~~ ~~~ ~~ ~~ ~~.

INTERNATIONAL
ARTIST SIGNS
CONTRACT FOR
CHURCH
WINDOWS----

~~~~ ~~~~~~ ~~
~~~ ~~ ~ ~~~~~ ~
~~ ~ ~~~ ~~~ ~
~~~ ~ ~~ ~~~~~
~~ ----.

~~~ ~~~~~ ~~ ~~~~
~~~~

MANY GREEK WOMEN, BOTH JEWISH
AND NON-JEWISH, BECOME FOLLOWERS.

FOLLOWERS GATHER HERE:

~~ ~~ ~~~ ~~~ ~~ ~~~ ~~ ~~
~~ ~~ ~~ ~~ ~ ~~~ ~ ~ ~~~ ~~.

JOB WANTED:
WOMAN LOOKING FOR GOOD-PAYING
JOB — HARDWORKING, EXPERIENCE
WITH ABACUS, SLIDE RULE, COMPUTER.
RESUMÉ AND REFERENCES.
CONTACT: SHARI 555-WORK

THIS WEEK 10 YEARS AGO...

MOTHER WAS
PRESENT AT
SON'S DEATH.

~~ ~~
~~~~ ~~~~~~
~~~ ~ ~~~
~~ ~~~~ ~~

WOMAN REPORTS
JESUS HAS RISEN
FROM THE DEAD!

~~~ ~~~ ~~~~~ ~~
~~ ~~ ~~~ ~~~~
~~~ ~~~~ ~~ ~ ~~.

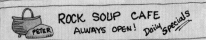

ROCK SOUP CAFE
PETER   ALWAYS OPEN! Daily Specials

The followers of Jesus shared their homes, food, and money with each other. One day a woman named Sapphira lied to Peter about how much money she had to share. Peter said to her, "How could you lie and put the Spirit of the Lord to the test?" With that, she died and was buried with her husband. **CAN YOU FIND SAPPHIRA?**

One day Paul and some other followers of Jesus went to the bank of a river to pray. There they met a woman named Lydia. She already loved God, so she became a follower of Jesus. After she was baptized, she invited some of Jesus' followers to stay at her house, which they did. **CAN YOU FIND LYDIA?**

Priscilla was a follower of Jesus who often held meetings in her house with other followers of the Lord. One day she met a man named Apollos. Apollos knew something about the Lord Jesus, but Priscilla took him to her house to teach him more about Jesus. **CAN YOU FIND PRISCILLA?**

The followers of Jesus taught his message in the synagogues and town squares of Greece. Many Jewish and non-Jewish women in the country came to believe in Jesus. **CAN YOU FIND THE WOMEN FOLLOWERS OF JESUS?**

ITALY ROME

ASIA

BIT

PAMPHYLIA

LYCIA

CORINTH

CRETE

CYP

SICILY

MALTA

PETER

COME AGAIN

Peter Carries God's Message to the Gentiles (People Who Weren't Jewish)

Jesus, and those who followed him while he was in the world, were Jews. After Jesus rose from the dead, God made it clear to the followers Jesus left behind, especially to Peter (see Acts 15:7-9), that he also wanted the *Gentiles* to be followers of Jesus.

Tabitha, who had become a follower of Jesus, got sick and died. Peter came and said, "Tabitha, stand up." She opened her eyes and got up. **CAN YOU FIND TABITHA?**

Peter found a crippled man living in Lydda. He told him, "Jesus Christ cures you. Get up." The man got up at once. **CAN YOU FIND THE CRIPPLED MAN?**

In Caesarea, there was a Gentile named Cornelius. Peter told Cornelius and his friends, "God doesn't favor any nation. Anyone who acts rightly is a friend of God's." **CAN YOU FIND CORNELIUS?**

Peter told Cornelius about Jesus. Then Cornelius and his friends were baptized and the Holy Spirit came upon them as tongues of fire. **CAN YOU COUNT THE TONGUES OF FIRE?**

Some of the Jewish followers of Jesus complained that Peter was baptizing Gentiles. Peter told them about Cornelius and they said, "Then God has granted life-giving forgiveness even to the Gentiles." **CAN YOU FIND PETER?**

In Jerusalem, Peter was arrested and put into jail. An angel appeared, broke his chains and freed him. **CAN YOU FIND THE ANGEL?**

Peter ended up in Rome. From there he sent letters on scrolls to Christians in places around the Mediterranean Sea. **CAN YOU FIND THE LETTERS?**

25

SEARCH 11

The Followers of Jesus Write His Story

About thirty years after Jesus rose from the dead, his followers began to write down his story. These writings make up the New Testament of the Bible. Most of the writers had known Jesus and wanted everyone else to be able to come to know Jesus.

 Matthew wrote about the day Jesus told a large crowd, "*Blessed* are those who show *mercy*; mercy shall be theirs." **CAN YOU FIND MATTHEW?**

Mark wrote a story about the day Jesus said, "Let the children come to me." **CAN YOU FIND MARK?**

 Luke tells us Jesus' story about a man who was beaten up. People saw him by the road, but left him there. Finally a man helped him. Jesus asked his followers, "Who acted like a neighbor to the hurt man?" Someone answered, "The man who helped him." Jesus then said, "Yes, and you are to do the same." **CAN YOU FIND LUKE?**

John wrote about the time Jesus compared himself to a grapevine. Jesus said that he is the trunk of the vine and each of his followers is one of the branches. **CAN YOU FIND JOHN?**

Peter wrote to the followers of Jesus and told them, "You are the living stones being built into the church of God." **CAN YOU FIND PETER?**

An unknown follower of Jesus wrote, "Love your fellow Christians always because you never know when you will be helping an angel." **CAN YOU FIND THE UNKNOWN WRITER?**

 Paul wrote that each follower of Jesus is a light in the world. He said that light leads to goodness and truth. **CAN YOU FIND PAUL?**

PETER

SEARCH 12

Those Who Knew Jesus Turn Over His Church to New Followers

By fifty years after he rose from the dead, most of the people who had known Jesus had died. If the Church Jesus had started with the help of the Apostles was going to survive, people who didn't know Jesus would have to come forward and be willing to live and die for him.

About seventy years after Jesus' Resurrection, a man named Ignatius was arrested for following Jesus. He wrote letters to his friends saying that he didn't mind dying because he would go to be with Jesus. **CAN YOU FIND IGNATIUS?**

A young woman named Perpetua was arrested for believing in Jesus. She said, "All things shall happen as God shall choose because we are all under the power of God." She was killed by *gladiators* for following Jesus. **CAN YOU FIND PERPETUA?**

A man named Clement ran a school in Egypt that taught about Jesus. Clement taught that rich people could follow Jesus so long as they used their money to help teach about Jesus. **CAN YOU FIND CLEMENT?**

Constantine, ruler of the Roman Empire, dreamed that the Christian God would help him win a battle. After he won the battle, Constantine ordered that people had to be allowed to follow Jesus if they wanted. **CAN YOU FIND CONSTANTINE?**

A few years later, Constantine's mother, Helen, went to Jerusalem to look for the cross of Jesus. **CAN YOU FIND HELEN?**

Now that people were free to follow Jesus, the light of truth Jesus had brought into the world could be spread by men, women and children to the ends of the earth. **CAN YOU FIND THE CHILDREN SPREADING THE LIGHT OF JESUS?**

SEARCH 13

The Message of Jesus is Passed From Follower to Follower

Since Jesus told his followers to teach everyone about him, millions of people have become followers of Jesus. Some spent their lives bringing God's message to people all over the world. These people are called missionaries.

 Patrick was born in England. He went to Ireland to teach about Jesus. **CAN YOU FIND PATRICK?**

Francis was born in the Italian city of Assisi. He cared for the poor. Today his followers teach about Jesus. **CAN YOU FIND FRANCIS OF ASSISI?**

 Francis Xavier was from Spain. He traveled from India to Japan teaching thousands of people about Jesus. **CAN YOU FIND FRANCIS XAVIER?**

Junipero Serra came to California from Spain to teach about Jesus. **CAN YOU FIND JUNIPERO SERRA?**

 Katharine Drexel was born in the United States in 1859. She taught minorities and other Americans about Jesus. **CAN YOU FIND KATHARINE DREXEL?**

William Sheppard was from the United States. In 1891, he went to Africa to teach people about Jesus. **CAN YOU FIND WILLIAM SHEPPARD?**

 Mother Teresa left her home in Europe to take the message of Jesus to India. **CAN YOU FIND MOTHER TERESA?**

Billy Graham traveled the world teaching about Jesus. **CAN YOU FIND BILLY GRAHAM?**

Karol Wojtyla was from Poland. After he became Pope John Paul II, he went all over the world teaching about Jesus. **CAN YOU FIND JOHN PAUL II?**

WELCOME TO OUR CHURCH DEDICATION!

PETER

Bibles

God Calls Us to Follow Him

Genesis 3:1-23; 12:1-5; Jonah 1:1-16; Matthew 3:13-17;
Luke 1:26-38; 2:41-50

1) After looking over the picture, explain to your child that the Old Testament is a series of stories about what happens to people when they do what God wants them to do, and what happens to them when they don't do what God wants. Point out that the reason God wants us to do some things and not do others is that he wants us to be happy. Discuss why parents tell their children to do some things (eat properly, brush their teeth and do their homework) and not do others (run into the street, ride a bike without a helmet and play with fire). Make clear that parents have such rules because they love their children. They don't want them to get hurt; they want them to be happy. Because we are God's children, he has rules for us because he loves us and wants what is best for us.

2) When you have found Jonah, point out that many other people in the Old Testament were called by God to do his work. Noah was called to build an ark to save his family and many animals from the great flood (see Genesis 6:11-22 and go back to the search to find Noah). Moses was called to lead God's people out of slavery in Egypt (see Exodus 3:4-10 and go back to the search to find Moses). Samuel was called by God to be a prophet (see 1 Samuel 3:1-10). Point out that these people did what God asked them to do (that is, they were faithful to God) and that, in return, God was faithful to them.

3) After finding Mary, explain that even though the angel's request was a strange one, Mary accepted it because it came from God. Mary had to accept many difficult things from Jesus—from God. As seen in the next search, she had to accept his running off to the Temple when he was twelve. When he was older, she had to accept his leaving home to roam the countryside preaching the word of God. After Jesus had been condemned, Mary had to accept his death as she watched from the foot of his cross. Explain that she accepted these difficult things because they came from God. Point out that, in return for her unquestioning acceptance of God's will, God took her to heaven to be with him forever.

4) Once your child has found Jesus in the Temple, discuss what young people in general can do to help Jesus accomplish the "Father's" work. They can study the Bible to learn what God expects of them. Certainly young people can pray—they can ask God to inspire them and others to be faithful to his call. Young people can donate a can of food a week to a food bank. They can perform acts of kindness and refrain from acts of unkindness. They can lead others to do God's work through their example. In all these things, young people will need the assistance and guidance of the older folks in their lives—their parents, grandparents, relatives and friends.

Jesus Calls His Disciples

Matthew 9:9; 19:16-22; Mark 1:16-18; Luke 6:12-16;
John 1:43-51

1) After looking at the picture, explain to your child that, in the time of Jesus, the Jewish people were ruled by the Romans. Because the Romans were harsh rulers, many Jews were expecting the promised Messiah (which means "deliverer") to arrive any day. These Jews expected the Messiah to come as an earthly king and "deliver" them from the power of the Romans. Explain that Jesus accepted the title "Messiah" (see Luke 9:18-20 and 24:46-48, and Matthew 16:15-20), but that he did not come to reestablish the Jewish Kingdom centered in Jerusalem. Rather he came to establish the "Kingdom of God" centered in peoples' hearts.

2) When you have found Peter and Andrew, point out to your child that these two men followed Jesus without asking for proof of his powers or divine origin—they followed him based on faith alone. As they followed Jesus and heard him preach and saw him heal the sick, they became his *disciples*, a word that means "pupils" or "learners." Further explain that Jesus' disciples wrote down in the Bible a lot of what Jesus said and did. Finally point out that we are to use the Bible to "learn" about Jesus so we, too, can become his disciples. Go over with your child the ways you both use the Bible to learn about Jesus. (This subject will be covered in greater detail in Search 11.)

3) After finding the "rich man," tell your child that even after learning about Jesus, some people decide not to follow him. The rich man decided not to follow Jesus because he didn't want to give away his money. Jesus points out that it will be difficult for the rich to enter heaven (see Matthew 19:21-23). Explain to your child that this isn't because having lots of stuff is bad in itself, it's because if we spend too much of our time getting and taking care of lots of stuff we probably won't have much time left to do what God wants us to do. Add up the excess hours you and your child spend each week on "stuff"—watching TV, playing on a computer, working too many hours, wandering around shopping malls or perfecting the lawn. Discuss some of the things you could do for God with some of these hours. Finally, tell your child that Jesus asked his followers, "What does it profit a man if he gains the whole world and suffers the loss of his soul?" Explain that the answer to this question is "Nothing!"

4) When you have found the twelve Apostles, explain that "twelve" was an important number for Jesus and the rest of the Jewish people. In Genesis 35:23-26, the twelve sons of Jacob are listed. Explain that the descendants of these twelve men became the twelve tribes of Israel. Finally connect the twelve tribes of Israel with the twelve Apostles by pointing out that there was one Apostle for each of the twelve tribes (see Matthew 19:28).

5) After completing the searches, go back to the picture and find the stone church that is beginning to be built. Show it to your child. Explain to your child that those first stones in the church building represent the first followers of Jesus. Further explain that it isn't the stones, or wood or steel or glass, that make a church, but the people who follow God. Point out that it is very important for God's followers to gather on Sundays and other days in church buildings to praise and worship God together. Explain that each piece of material that makes up our church buildings is representative of those who gather in that building to worship God. Get your child to imagine that one of the pieces of her church has her name on it. Finally, follow with your child the building of the church from page to page as more and more stones are added—as more people come to follow Jesus.

SEARCH 3

Jesus Gives His Message to His Followers
Matthew 6:5-13; 22:34-39; Luke 4:14-22; 14:12-14; 17:3-4; John 15:9-17; 21:15-17

1) After looking over the page, point out to your child the synagogue near the center of the picture. Explain that the "priest" or "minister" in a synagogue is called a *rabbi*, a word that means "teacher." In Jesus' time, the local town synagogues were the centers of learning. Jesus and his young friends would have gone regularly to their local synagogue to learn about God and their Jewish heritage. Discuss with your child some of the places you go to learn about God and your religious heritage—churches, museums, Christmas pageants, Easter sunrise services, Sunday school, prayer groups, Bible studies and religious schools.

2) Once you have found Jesus, explain that, by quoting this passage from the Old Testament, Jesus was saying that he had been sent by God to tell us what God wants us to do. Point out to your child that because Jesus is speaking for God, we should listen carefully to what he has to say. Also tell your child that, because God loves us, he would never do anything to hurt us, therefore anything he tells us to do must be good for us. If there has been some unhappiness in your family recently, such as the death of a relative, discuss this event with your child, pointing out that, even though the loss made you sad, as long as you maintain your faith in God, he will eventually turn all your sadness into joy. Why? Because he loves you.

3) When you have found the Man, explain that when Jesus tells us to love God, he is telling us to take some of the love God gives us and to give it back to God. Make clear that the kind of love God wants us to give him, and wants us to give one another, is not the kind you usually see on TV or in the movies. Review 1 Corinthians 13, especially verses 4-7. Then discuss some of the characteristics of the kind of love God gives us and wants in return, and that we are to share with one another—love that is patient, kind, truthful and bears all things. Explore with your child some of the ways you can demonstrate this kind of love. Next, tell your children about Mother Teresa, or another saint-like person with whom you are familiar. Point out that it is this kind of love—God's love—that makes it possible for saintly people to be happy in dedicating their lives to others. Finally, explain that when Jesus tells us to love God with our "minds," he is telling us to use our minds to help us do God's work and to help us to find God by studying the Bible and the world he has given us to live in.

4) After finding the partygoers, tell your child that Jesus was called a rabbi (or teacher) by his followers. Go over all the "teachers" in your child's life—parents, grandparents and other relatives, adult neighbors and friends, perhaps older brothers or sisters, priest, school teacher, and Sunday school teacher. Discuss how these teachers try to help your child. Explain that Jesus should always be considered her teacher and that the Bible is the textbook we should study to find out what God wants us to know and do.

5) When you have found Peter, have your child explain to you the importance of food to the human body. Then, explain that the human soul also needs food to stay healthy. Explain that when Jesus told Peter to feed his sheep, Jesus meant that Peter, as the leader of Jesus' followers, was to feed people's souls by teaching them what God wanted them to do. Point out that this command to Peter applies to all of us, and, if we love God, we will demonstrate our love by sharing God's word with our family, neighbors and friends. Explain that we do this in how we act, speak to, and treat each other. Make lists of actions that show our love for God and neighbor and actions that don't.

SEARCH 4

Jesus Sends His Followers Before Him
Matthew 10:1-42; Mark 6:7-13; Luke 9:1-6; 10:1-16

1) After finding Jesus, explain to your children that when the Jews to whom Jesus was talking heard the phrase "the Kingdom of God" they thought Jesus was saying that God was going to come to earth and become a king like those who ruled in many countries of the world. Jesus, however, meant something else. He meant he was going to show people how to set up the Kingdom of God inside themselves. Jesus was telling people that if they let God's spirit of love rule their hearts, minds, and actions, then the Kingdom of God would exist in them, and through them spread to others. Point out to your children some of the characteristics of people whose lives are ruled by God's love: they are generous, kind, forgiving, satisfied, caring and joyful. While it is rare to find one person who exhibits all these characteristics, try to identify people in your lives who exhibit one or more. Finally, help your children understand that people whose lives are ruled by God's love are happy in this world and get to spend eternity with God.

2) When you have found the "lost sheep," discuss with your children how easy it is for sheep to get lost if they don't have a shepherd. Sheep won't lose their way if they have someone to follow, but the minute they don't have a leader they begin to wander aimlessly, and get into trouble. By calling some of the "house of Israel" lost sheep, Jesus was saying that they had stopped following God and therefore were wandering aimlessly and getting into trouble. By sending his followers across the countryside, Jesus was letting the people know that God had sent a new shepherd for the people to follow (see John 10:1-16). Point out to your children that they will have many shepherds in their lives—parents, grandparents, teachers, priests, employers—that they will have to follow to one degree or another. Finally point out that over all these is God, whom we should try to follow as closely as possible because, if we do, God will never allow us to wander aimlessly or get into trouble.

3) After finding the twelve Apostles, explain to your children that the Apostles were preparing the way for Jesus to come after them (see Luke 13:22). Discuss the people who help prepare children for Jesus to come to them—parents and others who read religious books with them and are examples of God, other loving people, churches that have preserved the faith and teaching of Jesus, preachers who minister to and teach them, Sunday School teachers who guide them, and faith-filled people throughout history. Ask your children if they can think of anyone in particular who has helped them prepare for Jesus—to learn, think, and care about Jesus.

4) Finally, tell your children that some of Jesus' followers decided not to follow him anymore (see Matthew 19:16-22, John 6:60-69, John 10:31-39, and John 11:45-53). Explain that most who refused to follow Jesus did so because he made them uncomfortable. He either asked them to do something they didn't want to do, or told them to stop doing things they wanted to keep doing. Go over some of the things you tell your children to do and some you tell them not to do. Discuss whether your rules ever make your children feel uncomfortable. Point out that if some of the rules do make your children uncomfortable it's probably their occasional failure to carry out the rules that causes the discomfort and not the rules themselves. Explain that it is the same way with God's rules—it's usually not the rules themselves that make us uncomfortable to be around God, but our failure to do what we know God wants us to do that builds a wall between us and God, and we become lost.

SEARCH 5

Jesus Sends the Holy Spirit
to Help His Followers

Acts 1:1-9, 15-26; 2:1-39; 6:1-6

1) After reading the opening paragraph, explain to your child that some of the people who didn't like Jesus arrested him (see Matthew 26:47-56) and killed him (see Mark 15:21-37). Tell them that Jesus allowed himself to be killed to show how much he loved us and his Father in heaven. Further explain that after three days God raised Jesus from the dead (see Luke 24:1-12) and visited with his followers to encourage them to continue telling people about God (see John 20 and 21). Once you and your child have discussed these events, go back to the picture and find the scenes that depict the crucifixion and resurrection of Jesus.

2) When you have found Mathias, explain to your child that by choosing someone to replace Judas as one of the Apostles, the leaders of the early Church (those who had personally known Jesus) were demonstrating that they had the authority to choose new leaders of the Church. Later on this page you will search for seven men whom the Apostles chose to be members of the priesthood of Jesus' Church. The Apostles placed their hands on these men to show that they had become servants of God. Explain to your child that during the sacrament of ordination, a bishop—a modern-day leader of the Church—will place his hands on the new priest to show that he has become a servant of God.

3) After counting the tongues of fire, tell your child that the tongues were how the Holy Spirit chose to show himself. Remind your child that the Holy Spirit is the power of the love that flows between God the Father and God the Son, and between the Father and the Son and their creation. Explain how important it is that we ask God to send his spirit of love to us and that we open our hearts and minds to receive it. Finally explain that fire is a symbol of cleansing and action. This means that when the Holy Spirit entered Jesus' followers, it cleansed their hearts and minds and led them into the streets to tell all the people about Jesus. This spirit is still helping the followers of Jesus and will help them until the end of time.

4) When you have found the Apostles, point out to your child that the people the Apostles were talking to were Jews who had come to Jerusalem from many different countries. Explain that the Jews were the "chosen people of God"—the people who God guided throughout the Old Testament. The Apostles presented Jesus to these Jews as the Messiah—the deliverer promised to the Jewish people in the Old Testament. This is the way Jesus presented himself (see Luke 9:18-20 and John 7:25-31). As the Messiah, Jesus brought his message first to God's chosen people. As the followers of Jesus, his Apostles did the same. Explain to your child that, though Jesus brought his message first to the Jews, he intended his message for all the people in the world. Finally explain that after the Apostles taught Jesus' message to the Jews, they began to teach it to anyone they came across. The rest of the searches in this book make this clear.

SEARCH 6

Jesus Calls Saul to Be
His Follower

Acts 4:1-10; 7:54-60; 8:3; 9:3-5, 10-22

1) After finding Peter, explain to your children that people are persecuted, or simply treated unfairly or unkindly, for many different reasons: for what they believe; for what they look like; for where they are from; for what they do or don't do. Point out that Jesus would not have liked such behavior. Explain that regardless of what people may think or do, or what they look like or where they are from, God tells us that we must love them. This doesn't mean that all actions and beliefs are pleasing to God, but it means that what a person does or is doesn't free us from the obligation to love them. It doesn't give us the right to decide who is worthy of our love and who is not. Finally, explain the difference between liking a person and loving a person (see 1 Corinthians 13) and that when we love a person, we are loving the spirit of God within them and not necessarily what they do or are.

2) After finding Saul for the first time, explain to your children that Jesus was seen as a threat to the status quo. Throughout history many followers of Jesus, such as Francis of Assisi and Joan of Arc, and other people, such as abolitionists, labor leaders, pacifists and environmentalists, have also been seen as threats to the status quo. Point out to your children that even though many people who have struggled to make the world a better place have had a difficult time, the world is indeed a better place. Further explain that we are not responsible for making the world a better place, but we are responsible for *trying* to make it a better place. Whether we succeed or not is up to God. Finally point out that, because we are only expected by God to try to make the world a better place, we should not be afraid to make the effort.

3) When you have found the preaching Saul, tell your children that his preaching was a direct result of his "seeing" that whenever he hurt one of the followers of Jesus, he was actually hurting Jesus himself. Just as when we love someone, we are loving the spirit of God within that person, when we hurt someone, we are hurting that same spirit of God. Explain that if we "see" the spirit of God in the people around us we will, like the "seeing" Saul, reach out to them and "love them as ourselves."

4) Next, explain that the persecution of the followers of Jesus in Jerusalem forced many of them to leave Jerusalem and travel to other, and safer, cities. If your Bible has a map of the Mediterranean area, point out some of the cities where the followers of Jesus went (Antioch, Corinth, Athens, Malta and Rome). Explain that this helped Jesus' followers spread his teachings. Also explain that the teachings of Jesus are still being spread around the world today. Point out some of the ways this is happening: through the work of missionaries, by the written word, by radio and television. Finally, discuss some of the ways you and your children might do your bit to try, as followers of Jesus, to spread his teachings—by praying and reading the Bible together, by going to church, by wearing a religious symbol, by being good examples to those around you, by loving your neighbor and by sharing the word of Jesus.

The Followers of Jesus
Travel to Antioch

Acts 11:19-26; 13:1-31; 5:22-35

1) After looking over the picture, look at the inside cover. Show your child where Antioch is in relation to Jerusalem. Explain that the leaders in Jerusalem were attacking the followers of Jesus in an attempt to stop people from teaching about Jesus. The results of the attacks, however, had the opposite effect. Because Jesus' followers found Jerusalem a very dangerous place to stay, they left and scattered from Egypt all the way to Rome. As they traveled, they spread the very teachings the leaders of Jerusalem were trying to wipe out.

2) When you have located Barnabas, ask your child if she thinks the followers of Jesus who left Jerusalem had to give up a lot. Of course they did. Certainly many left behind friends, relatives, homes and their jobs. Point out to your child that often people who believe in something, or who stand for good and decent things, are asked to give up something for their beliefs. Review some of the characters in the Old Testament who gave up things because God asked them to: Abraham, who gave up his home at God's call; Noah, who built the Ark at the command of God; Moses, who left his home and family to follow God to Egypt. Finally, remind your child that Jesus gave up his life for us because God, his Father, told him to.

3) After you have found the messengers, remind your child that they came from Jerusalem, where Peter and some of the other Apostles remained. Explain that when the argument broke out over whether or not non-Jewish followers of Jesus had to obey all Jewish laws, the Christians in Antioch asked Peter and the rest of the church leaders in Jerusalem to decide the issue (see Acts 15:1-35). After discussing the issue, Peter and the rest of the Apostles decided that, since God was allowing the Holy Spirit to flow into the non-Jewish followers of Jesus (see Acts 8:14-17), the non-Jewish followers of Jesus should not be required to obey all Jewish laws.

4) After finding Barnabas and Saul, explain that by laying their hands on these two men, the church leaders in Antioch, through the power of the Holy Spirit, brought Barnabas and Saul into the priesthood of Jesus (see Acts 8:14-18). Further explain that all those baptized into the Church of Jesus become part of the "royal priesthood" and, as such, are responsible for spreading the word of God and living a Christ-like life (see 1 Peter 2:4-10). Review with your child some of the ways to do these things—read and study the Bible, be a good example, pray often, share with those in need and participate in church activities.

Paul Spreads
God's Message

Acts 13:4-11; 14:8-10; 16:25-31; 17:22-25; 18:7-11; 28:1-6, 17-20

1) Before doing the searches, go around the border of the map with your child. If you have an atlas, and your child is old enough, find a map of this area and show your child how this area of the world looks when exactly rendered. Next show your child the maps in the back of your Bible, if you have them. If your child has done some traveling and has a sense of distance, relate the distances Paul traveled to a trip you have taken. Finally, discuss with your child how much harder and slower it was for Paul to travel than it is for us—he had to walk or ride a horse or go on small and dangerous boats.

2) After looking over the page, tell your child that Saul began to be called Paul in the Acts of the Apostles for no apparent reason (see Acts 13:9). Ask your child if she has any idea why someone might want to change his name. Could it be that Saul was trying to hide from something? Maybe he had become ashamed of how he had treated the followers of Jesus—driving them from their homes and putting them in prison. Or maybe Saul wanted a new name to go with his new love of Jesus. Tell your child that at Confirmation people add a new name to their current name—the name of a holy follower of Jesus. Explain that the person whose name they pick is a guide they choose to help them to grow closer to Jesus.

3) When you have found the blind magician, explain to your child that Paul's missionary journeys were mainly to his fellow Jews who were living all around the Mediterranean Sea. Since the Jews were the people God had prepared to receive the Messiah, it makes sense that the Jews should have been the first ones to know that he had come into the world. Also remind your child that all of the early followers of Jesus were Jews and that, therefore, early Christianity was considered a continuation of the Jewish faith tradition—at least by the Jews who had become followers of Jesus. Explain that, for this reason, the early followers of Jesus thought you had to be a Jew to be a follower of Jesus and that you also had to continue to follow Jewish rules and traditions even after you became a follower of Jesus. Later this changed, as you will see in the search about Peter's missionary journeys (see Search 10).

4) After finishing the search, ask your child if she thinks that Paul, even with the help of Barnabas, could teach all the people in the area about Jesus. Certainly he couldn't. Next ask what your child thinks Paul did about the new followers of Jesus he left behind when he left a town. Explain that he did two things. First he, or another Church leader, appointed new leaders to lead the local community of "Christians" (see Acts 6:1-7 and Titus 1:5-9). In addition, he wrote letters to the "Christians" he left behind further explaining the teachings of Jesus and encouraging the new followers of Jesus to be faithful to the word of God (see Search 11).

SEARCH 9

Many Women Answer the Call of Jesus to Follow Him

Matthew 28:1-10; John 19:25-27; Acts 5:1-10; 9:36-37; 12:6-16; 16:13-15; 18:24-26; 1 Corinthians 16:19

1) Before beginning the page, point out to your children that Jesus often reached out to and responded to women during his public ministry. The first miracle he performed in public was in response to a request from his mother (see John 2:1-11). When Jesus found Peter's mother-in-law sick, he immediately took her by the hand and cured her (see Mark 1:29-31). He also raised a Jewish leader's daughter from the dead (see Matthew 9:18-26) and cured a non-Jewish woman's daughter when she called out to him (see Matthew 15:27-28). Jesus also forgave the sins of the woman who washed his feet with her tears (see Luke 7:36-50). Finally, explain that Jesus, almost at the moment of his death, was thinking of his mother when he asked a friend of his to take care of her (see John 19:25-27). Explain that Jesus understood that God values men and women equally because, as we are told in Genesis 1:27, "God created man in his image; male and female he created them."

2) After finding Jesus' mother, Mary, explain that surely she didn't want her son to die. She must have asked God to spare her son from death. Point out that if ever there was a prayer that deserved to be answered, this appears to be it. But God had other plans. While it seemed to Mary that her son's death made no sense, it appeared otherwise to God. Explain to your children that it's often the same with our prayers. We ask God for something we think is good for us, but don't get it because God has other plans: plans that we have no way of knowing. Point out that parents play a similar role in their young children's lives. Infants want to put keys in electric sockets, but parents say no; young children want to ride bikes without helmets or ride in cars without seat belts, but parents say no; older kids want to drive cars without proper training, but again parents say no. Finally, explain that just as one day kids come to understand their parents' responses to their requests, one day we will understand God's responses to our prayers.

3) After finding Sapphira, explain that she lost her life, not just because she lied, but because she lied to God. Point out that the first lie she told wasn't to Peter, but to herself. Before she lied to Peter, she had to tell herself it would be OK to hold back some of her money. If she had not died, she would have had to continue to lie to cover up her first lies. To help your children understand how lies build upon lies, tell them this story: A child was told to eat a piece of chicken, but fed it to her dog instead. When asked if she ate the chicken, the child said yes. Then the dog began to choke, and when the child was asked if she knew why, she said no. At the vet's, the parents were told that unless a simple explanation for the choking could be discovered, the dog would have to undergo a dangerous operation. And there stood the child, in a very difficult trap made of lies.

4) When you have counted the women followers of Jesus, explain that, because women were not as involved as men were in governmental, religious or commercial work, they were freer to commit to Jesus than were many men. Because Jesus and his teachings were unpopular among many government, religious and economic leaders, men who depended upon these leaders for their livelihood were reluctant to follow Jesus, at least publicly. Finally, explain that many women of Jesus' time found in him a sense of belonging, of being loved, and of being important. These are the same things each of us is seeking and many are still finding in Jesus today.

SEARCH 10

Peter Carries God's Message to the Gentiles (People Who Weren't Jewish)

Acts 9:36-43; 10:24-36, 44-48; 11:11-18; 12:1-11; 1 Peter 1:1-2

1) After reading the opening paragraph, read Acts 15:1-35. It describes the meeting in Jerusalem at which the Apostles formally decided that Gentiles could become followers of Jesus without having to agree to follow all of the Jewish laws. Explain to your child that up to this time almost all the followers of Jesus had been Jews, like Jesus himself was. Naturally, the Jewish followers of Jesus assumed that to become a follower of a Jewish religious teacher—Jesus—you would first have to accept the teachings of the Jewish religion. The Apostles, who had known Jesus, decided, with the help of the Holy Spirit, that this was not the case. Finally, remind your children that Jesus himself reached out to non-Jews (see Mark 7:24-30, Luke 10:25-37, and John 4:4-10).

2) After finding Tabitha, tell your child that God gave Peter the power to raise Tabitha from the dead for at least three reasons. First, at his ascension, Jesus promised his Apostles that he would always be with them (see Matthew 28:20). Clearly the power to raise someone from the dead was a sign to Peter that God was still with him. Second, such a powerful sign was useful to the Apostles in carrying out their job of convincing people to follow Jesus (see Acts 9:42). Finally, Jesus had said that he was the resurrection and the life and that whoever believed in him would never die (see John 11:21-26). Tabitha's resurrection from the dead was certainly a strong sign that Jesus is the resurrection and the life.

3) When you have counted the tongues of fire, remind your child that the Holy Spirit, as promised by Jesus (see Acts 1:8), had come upon the Apostles (see Acts 2:1-4 and Search 5). At the time the Holy Spirit came upon the Apostles, it made sense for them to assume that it did so because they were Jewish followers of the Jewish Messiah. Explain that even though Jesus had made it clear that he had come to bring salvation to all people, not only Jews (see Matthew 28:18-19), God still sent the Holy Spirit upon Cornelius and the other Gentiles to make it clear that the saving power of Jesus was meant for everyone, everywhere.

4) When you have counted the letters, review with your child the idea of priesthood. For the Jewish people, the position of "priest" was reserved for a select few, whose responsibility was to teach and preserve the laws of God (see 1 Samuel 2:35). As the selected followers of Jesus, the Apostles saw themselves as the "priests" of the new branch of Judaism that came to be called Christianity. Their job was to teach and preserve the laws of God as revealed by Jesus. As the Apostles traveled around and led more people to Jesus, they ordained other people as "priests" and left them in the villages they had visited (see Acts 6:1-6 and Acts 14:23). Finally, explain that all baptized followers of Jesus are members of his priesthood (see 1 Peter 2:4-9), and as such are responsible for teaching and preserving the laws of God that Jesus taught to his first followers.

SEARCH 11

The Followers of Jesus
Write His Story

Matthew 5:7; Mark 10:13-14; Luke 6:36-38; 10:25-37;
John 15:1-5; Ephesians 5:8-9; Hebrews 13:1-2; 1 Peter 2:4-5

1) After finding Matthew, point out to your child that, when the Jews Jesus was talking to saw him on the side of a mountain explaining the laws of God to them, they would have thought of Moses, who was the great lawgiver of the Old Testament (see Exodus 32:15-16). Explain that Jesus often referred to the Old Testament because the people he was talking to were very familiar with it, so the references Jesus made helped them understand what he was saying. Tell your child that, in the same way, our knowledge of the Old Testament will help us understand what Jesus is trying to say to us. Finally, go over the Beatitudes from the Sermon on the Mount (see Matthew 5:1-12). Use examples from your life and your child's life that might help your child understand the difficult ideas of sorrow, meekness, holiness and peace-keeping.

2) After finding Luke, tell your child that this story is called the story of the "Good Samaritan." Point out that the man who stopped and helped the man who had been beaten up was a Samaritan. Explain that the Jewish people looked down on Samaritans and thought they were a people unworthy of the love of God. Jews, therefore, usually had nothing to do with them. In his story, Jesus had a Samaritan stop and help the injured man because he wanted to make it clear to his Jewish listeners that anyone who does what God asks of him pleases God and is God's friend. Finally, explain that the Samaritan helped the man without considering whether or not the man was deserving of his help. Make it clear to your child that God also expects us to help people without considering whether they deserve our help. Whether someone in need deserves our help is God's business, not ours.

3) When you have found John, tell your child how a tree (or vine) lives. Explain that the roots of the tree are under the ground, that they feed the tree and keep it safely anchored in the ground. Next, the trunk, or the main part of the tree, holds the branches of the tree up above the ground so the tree's leaves will be in the sun and grow. Explain that in the story John tells us, Jesus is saying that he is the main part of the tree—the roots and trunk. He is telling us that if we stick with him he will keep us firmly anchored in this life, and hold us up so that we can grow towards living with him when we leave this world. Finally point out that if you cut a branch off a tree it will die, just as we would if we cut ourselves off from God completely.

4) After finding Peter, explain to your child that the real "church" of God consists of all his followers (the English word "church" comes from the Greek word *kyraikos*, meaning "belonging to the Lord"). Explain that we have buildings that we call churches so we will have a place to gather with other followers of the Lord to praise God and to share and strengthen our faith. Imagine with your child what part of your church building you might like to be, or think you are most like. Finally, point out that because the real Church is made up of all those who follow the Lord, that all those in heaven are also, along with the Lord's followers on earth, members of his "church."

SEARCH 12

Those Who Knew Jesus Turn Over
His Church to New Followers

1) After looking over the search, tell your child that this page is about the followers of Jesus who never met him while he was in the world. Explain that these people were very important because, if they hadn't come forward to continue spreading Jesus' message, Jesus would have been quickly forgotten. Just like you and your child, these men and women had to believe in Jesus based on what they read about him or were told about him. Tell your children that believing in something you don't see is called having "faith" in that something. Tell them the story of "doubting Thomas" (see John 20:24-29). Point out that when Jesus said to Thomas, "Blest are they who have not seen and have believed," he was talking about all those people who would live after he had left the world, but would still believe in him even though they had never seen him. Point out that we believe in many things we cannot see—like radio and television waves, gravity and electrons. Finally, tell your child that, just as we have evidence for the existence of these things we don't see but believe in, we have evidence for the existence of God: everything in the universe.

2) After finding Perpetua, tell your children that people like Perpetua and Ignatius, who are willing to die for what they believe in, are called martyrs (see Luke 12:1-21 and Matthew 5:11-12). Explain that the martyrs who died for Jesus were very important in keeping his memory alive in the world. Every time someone died for Jesus, many other people would begin to wonder what it was about Jesus that made people willing to die for him. Eventually many of these people became followers of Jesus. Explain that while dying for Jesus is an extreme case of leading by example, each of us is expected to try living for Jesus. Review with your child ways we can do this—by praying both in private and in public, through acts of kindness to family members and strangers, by showing gratitude to God for the gift of life, by praising God in church with other followers of Jesus and by seeking to do God's will at all times. Finally, make it clear to your children that we are not responsible for always succeeding at all these tasks, but we are responsible for trying.

3) When you have found the children with torches, explain to your child that, as wonderful and important as living, and even dying, for Jesus is, it is our believing, our faith in the saving power of Jesus' love for us, that will eventually bring us to heaven to be with him (see John 11:25-26, Mark 5:25-34, and Acts 15:11). Once your child understands that it is our faith in the saving power of God that brings us eternal life, discuss with them the actions such a faith naturally leads to. Point out that if we really believe God loves us and sent his son to die for us, we will be unable to stop doing the things God wants us to do. Point out that the people in this search, who lived and died for Jesus, did so in response to their faith that Jesus lived and died for them. Lastly, make sure your child understands that faith is sufficient for salvation, but that a true faith in the love of God will always lead to good action (see James 2:14-26).

The Message of Jesus Is Passed
From Follower to Follower

1) After looking over the picture, discuss with your child the meaning of being a missionary. Explain that anyone who teaches someone about Jesus is a missionary. Point out that teaching about Jesus includes a wide range of activities, from studying the Bible with someone; to going to a senior's home to visit with elderly people; to spending your entire life traveling around the world telling people about Jesus. Explain that at one time or another in our lives, we all act as missionaries. Those who regularly attend church are teaching, through example, about God's call to praise and worship him. Any follower of Jesus who does the right thing in a difficult situation is, through example, teaching about Jesus, and therefore is a missionary. Most Christian churches encourage members to visit the sick, to help stock food pantries for the poor, to participate in pro-life activities, and so on. Many Christian churches go so far as to encourage their members, young and old, to actually go to a foreign country for periods of a few weeks to up to a year, to teach about Jesus. Finally, help your child to see the times when he has acted as a missionary for Jesus.

2) After finding Mother Teresa, explain to your child that missionaries like Mother Teresa encouraged many other people to become followers of Jesus and to become missionaries themselves. Mother Teresa started a community of sisters for the thousands of women who wanted to help her. They are called the Missionaries of Charity. Likewise, Katharine Drexel founded a community called the Sisters of the Blessed Sacrament. Francis of Assisi founded an order of priests and brothers called the Franciscans. A Canadian missionary, Marguerite Bourgeoys, founded a religious community called the Congregation of Notre Dame. People like these did much in their own lives to teach about Jesus and left behind large groups of people to carry on the Lord's work. Most of us are never going to start religious communities, but remind your child that each of us is responsible for being a missionary for Jesus in our everyday actions. Finally, explain to your child that, even though we don't always know the effect our actions have on people, our simple acts of goodness and kindness have a long-term effect on those we meet.

3) When you have finished the searches, go over the picture and find the children carrying torches. They are carrying the light of Jesus wherever they go. Explain to your child that, as a baptized member of the family of Jesus, she needs to keep her "candle" lit as she goes about her everyday life. Read to her the story of Samuel (see 1 Samuel 3:1-10). In this story, Samuel, who is a young boy, is called by God. At first, Samuel doesn't understand that it is God who is calling him. He thinks he is being called by Eli, a priest in the Temple. After Samuel comes to Eli the second time, Eli understands that it is God calling the young boy, and explains to Samuel what is going on. Tell your child that she, and all other people, are like Samuel—at some time in her life God will call her. When this happens, it will be helpful to your child if there is someone in her life—you, a friend or relative, a pastor or a teacher—who can fulfill the role of Eli and help your child respond to the call of God just as Samuel did, by saying, "Speak, Lord, for your servant is listening."

Glossary

Altar—A raised platform where offerings are made to God.

Apostle—Someone who is a "messenger." Jesus picked twelve apostles from among his many disciples to lead in carrying God's message to the world.

Baptize—To clean and set aside for God. Water is used in the ceremony to show that the person being baptized is being cleansed by God and born again to God.

Bishop—A servant of the Lord who is responsible for teaching people the rules of God.

Blessed—Made happy or holy.

Commandment—An order to do or not to do something.

Crucifixion—A Roman punishment that resulted in the death of a person nailed to a cross.

Crusade—An enthusiastic undertaking in the name of some specific cause, such as spreading the teachings of Jesus.

Damascus—One of the major cities in the area where Jesus lived, about one hundred miles from Jerusalem.

Dedication—The setting aside of something for a special and specific purpose. Churches are set aside as places for the special and specific purpose of worshipping and praising God.

Descendants—All the people in your family who come after you.

Disciple—A pupil or follower of a teacher. Jesus had many disciples when he was in the world. Anyone who follows Jesus today is one of his disciples.

Disobey—To refuse to do what you are told to do.

Gentile—A non-Jewish person; anyone who was not a Jew.

Gladiator—A man who fought against animals or other men. They fought in sports arenas for the amusement of the spectators. They were often used to kill early followers of Jesus.

Hallowed—Made holy or honored as sacred.

Heaven—The name Christians give to our way of being with God forever, even after death.

Holy Spirit—The active presence of God in our life; God's love shared with us.

House of Israel—All the *descendants* of Israel, whose twelve sons were the fathers of the twelve tribes of Israel (see Genesis 35:23-26); also called the Israelites.

Jewish People—Any *descendants* of God's chosen people—also called Hebrews or Israelites. The Jewish people were the descendants of the twelve sons of Israel, each of whom founded one of the twelve tribes of Israel (see Genesis 35:9-26).

Kingdom of God—Any place where God's love rules.

Lord—Someone who has great power. God is often called "the Lord."

Lost Sheep—The Israelites who had stopped following God.

Mercy—Not punishing someone as much as he might deserve to be punished.

Messiah—The person sent by God to free his people. At the time of Jesus, many Jews were waiting for God to send them a king who would free them from their Roman rulers. Many Jews thought Jesus was this special person.

Miracle—An unusual event, such as water turning into wine, that doesn't happen in nature and is therefore considered to be caused by God.

Missionary—Anyone who spreads the word of God as he goes through his life, but especially someone who leaves his home and goes to a new place to teach about God.

Nineveh—A city in ancient Assyria, along the Tigris river, about six hundred miles from Jerusalem.

Obey—To do what you are asked or commanded to do.

Old Testament—The Jewish holy books that tell the story of creation and of man's relationship to God.

Pentecost—The Jewish Feast of Weeks (see Exodus 34:22). During this feast, the Jewish people thanked God for the harvest. It was on this feast day that the Holy Spirit was sent by God to the Apostles (see Acts 2:1-4).

Prophet Isaiah—A prophet is a person who speaks for God. Isaiah was one of the prophets who told the Jewish people that God was going to send his son to them.

Roman Empire—The land around the Mediterranean Sea that was ruled from the Italian city of Rome for hundreds of years, including the time of Jesus.

Scroll—A rolled-up piece of animal skin or paper that has writing on it.

Sea of Galilee—A large lake in the area where Jesus lived—about twelve miles from Nazareth. Some of the twelve Apostles were fishermen on this lake.

Spirit of the Lord—Commonly called the Holy Spirit, it is the active presence of God in our lives; God's love shared with us.

Synagogue—A Jewish "church" where Jews go to learn about, praise and worship God.

Temple—A building where Jesus' people worshiped God. The Wailing Wall, what remains of the Jerusalem Temple, is still the most holy place for the Jewish people.

Ten Commandments—The basic rules for living that God gave to Moses on Mount Sinai to pass on to God's chosen people (see Exodus 20:1-17).

Tomb—A cave or building where people's bodies are placed after they die.

Tongues of Fire—The Holy Spirit looked like flames when it came down on the disciples on Pentecost.

Bering Sea

ALASKA

Hudson Bay

GREENLAND

ICEL

NORTH AMERICA

Atlantic Ocean

Pacific Ocean

HAWAII

CENTRAL AMERICA

NEW WORLDS

SOUTH AMERICA